EXTINCT! CREATURES OF THE PAST

by Mary Batten

illustrated by Beverly Doyle

To my son, Robert, with love
M.B.

The illustrations in this book are dedicated to
the animal species threatened with extinction
B.D.

Special thanks to Christopher Shaw,
George C. Page Museum; Donald McNamee, Natural
History Museum of Los Angeles County; Stephen Wroe,
University of New South Wales; and my creative editor
Jennifer Dussling, whose idea sparked this book.

Library of Congress Cataloging-in-Publication
Batten, Mary.
Extinct! : creatures of the past / by Mary Batten ; illustrated by Beverly Doyle.
        p.   cm. — (Road to reading. Mile 4)
Summary: Describes giant bugs, birds, and mammals that lived long ago and
became extinct during the last Ice Age, discusses the extinction of more
recent animals, and examines the effort to protect endangered species.
ISBN: 0-307-46405-9 (GB) — ISBN: 0-307-26405-X (pbk.)
1. Extinct animals—Juvenile literature. 2. Animals, Fossil—Juvenile litera-
ture. [1. Prehistoric animals. 2. Extinct animals. 3. Extinction (Biology)]
I. Doyle, Beverly, 1963- ill. II. Title. III. Series.

QE765 .B38 2000
560—dc21   00-027013
                                                      CIP

A GOLDEN BOOK • New York
Golden Books Publishing Company, Inc. New York, New York 10106

ISBN 0-307-26405-X (pbk)   A MM
ISBN 0-307-46405-9 (GB)

Contents

1
Gone Forever

The sun rises over grassy plains. In the distance, a huge shape lumbers across the ground. Slowly it moves closer and closer. It has hoofed feet like a horse. Its neck is as long as a giraffe's. Its head is as large as a person. And its body is as big as a house!

This bizarre animal is a hornless rhino. It is the largest land mammal that ever lived.

Where can you see hornless rhinos? You can't. Not ever. They don't live in zoos or anyplace else on Earth. The last ones died off millions of years ago. They went extinct. Once an animal becomes extinct, it can never come back.

Nothing lasts forever. Not animals, not plants, not mountains, not even stars. Life is always coming and going. The kinds of animals on Earth today are not all the animals that ever lived.

At least one hundred times this many have lived during Earth's long history.

How old is Earth? Very, very, very old—four and a half billion years old. It's hard to imagine so much time.

Life is also very old. There has been life on Earth for at least three and a half billion years. The earliest living things were bacteria. Bacteria are small, simple forms of life. They can be seen only through a microscope.

People are some of the newest animals on the planet. We are only about two million years old. In between bacteria and people came an incredible number of animals. We know about these ancient creatures because of the fossils they left behind.

Fossils are the remains of animals and plants. Sometimes when an animal dies, it is buried in clay or sand before it rots away. Over time, the sand or clay hardens around the bones. They turn to stone. Fossil comes from a Latin word meaning "dug up." Most fossils are dug up from rock.

We know about extinct animals from fossil skulls, skeletons, and teeth. The most famous animals that became extinct are the dinosaurs. But there

were many others—strange, bizarre
creatures—that walked this world
years and years ago.

2
Big Bugs

Earth's first forests were warm and wet. Forests today are filled with leafy trees. Forests back then had tall horsetail plants and spindly trees. There were no flowers, but there were lots of gigantic ferns.

Bugs were also gigantic. A cockroach the size of a grown-up's hand scurried along a rotting tree trunk. Overhead, a giant dragonfly as big as a seagull flew through the air.

Meanwhile, on the ground, a spider hunted for food. Its body was the size

of a dinner plate. With its legs stretched out, it was eight feet across. Slowly, quietly, the spider crept up on a millipede. The millipede had two hundred pairs of legs and a body as long as a cow's.

Does this sound like something from a scary movie? It isn't. Long before the dinosaurs, animals that are tiny today, like spiders and insects, were huge. It was a great time for giant bugs because there weren't many other animals around to eat them. Of course, some bugs hunted and ate each other.

The time of the giant bugs lasted about 100 million years. Then the weather got colder and drier. The huge insects became extinct.

Still, their smaller cousins are almost everywhere today. Bugs live on every continent, from the hottest, driest desert in Africa to the frozen land of Antarctica.

3
Monster Birds

Millions of years after the giant
insects became extinct, dinosaurs
ruled the earth. They were around a
long time—almost 150 million years.
Toward the end of that time, some
small dinosaurs even had feathers.

Believe it or not, dinosaurs are
related to birds. Some scientists think

birds are really modern-day dinosaurs. Just think of that the next time you see a chicken!

Long before birds like chickens and crows and sparrows lived, there were *giant* birds. They could not fly. After the dinosaurs died out, they were the top predators.

One of these birds, called *Diatryma* (DI-uh-TRY-ma), stood nine feet tall. It had a head as big as a horse's. It had powerful dinosaur-like legs.

Diatryma may have been just a bird, but it was pretty fierce. It ran down its prey, pouncing on the animal

with claws outstretched. Then, with its
beak, this giant bird snapped a bone in
the animal's neck.

What kind of animals did *Diatryma*
feed on? Probably small reptiles and
mammals. Maybe even horses. At that
time, horses were no bigger than dogs!

Diatryma died off millions of years before people lived. But there is one kind of giant bird that was around as recently as two thousand years ago— the elephant bird. These birds lived on the island of Madagascar when people first got there.

Elephant bird eggs are the largest bird eggs known. Each one was about the size of a two-gallon bucket. A single egg could hold 7 ostrich eggs, 183 chicken eggs, or more than 12,000 hummingbird eggs!

Scientists think that people made the elephant birds extinct. People raided their nests and stole the eggs. They used the eggs for food and the eggshells as containers. Fewer baby birds hatched. Then the old birds died off, and there weren't enough new birds to take their place.

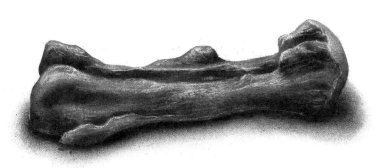

4
Giant Mammals

Mammals are animals that give
birth to live young, and make milk
to nurse their babies. People are
mammals. So are cats, dogs, bears,
monkeys, and lots of other animals.

When dinosaurs ruled the earth,
most mammals were no bigger than
mice. The sound or smell of a dinosaur

sent them scurrying into hiding. But after the dinosaurs became extinct, mammals came out of the shadows.

Over millions of years, mammals evolved into many more different species. Some grew larger and larger.

They became giants.

Great *Brontotherium* (BRON-toe-theer-ee-um), animals larger than modern rhinos, locked horns in fierce battles. A *Brontotherium* had crazy horns. They looked like a **V** on its nose.

Even pigs came in giant sizes. The "terrible pig" *Dinohyus* (DI-no-HI-us) was nine feet long and had wolflike teeth. It was a fierce fighter.

Glyptodon (GLIP-toe-dahn) was a ten-foot-long armadillo. It had a thick bony tail. It probably used its tail to fight off enemies.

In Australia, giant wombats and other strange animals appeared. They lived no place else on Earth. This is because Australia is an island. It was cut off from other lands by the ocean.

Imagine a steamy rain forest in northern Australia fifteen million years ago. A little bandicoot cries out as a huge animal with razor-sharp teeth jumps on it. The killer is a giant rat-kangaroo.

Did a giant rat-kangaroo have a pouch? Yes. Did it bounce on two legs like a kangaroo today? No. It probably walked on all four legs.

From looking at fossils, scientists think rat-kangaroos ate both meat and plants. They were probably the terrors of the forest for millions of years. Then they became extinct.

By that time, the earth had begun cooling again. It was the start of the last ice age. As Earth grew colder, even more animals grew larger.

Some scientists think getting bigger helped the animals survive. The thick layers of fat kept them warm. And keeping warm was not easy. Great ice sheets called glaciers locked much of Earth in a deep freeze.

5
Wild and Woolly

It is bitterly cold. Ice and snow are
everywhere. Inside a cave, women and
children huddle around a fire. Outside,
the men and older boys hunt for food.
They see a woolly mammoth.

Hunting a mammoth is dangerous. It
takes lots of skill. The animal is huge.
Its sharp, pointed tusks are thirteen feet

long. It weighs as much as 130 people!

The hunters circle their prey. They take aim and hurl their spears. Some pierce the animal's thick skin. The mammoth turns. The hunters run to escape the wounded beast. Finally, the mammoth falls. The hunters are happy. The mammoth will provide plenty of food. Its thick, shaggy fur will make warm clothing.

A mammoth's fur was made up of hairs as much as three feet long. It protected the animal from the freezing weather of the Ice Age.

Scientists know more about the

mammoth than any other extinct prehistoric mammal. Unlike fossils of other long-gone animals, many mammoth fossils are more than just bones. Some have flesh, hair, and even skin. This is because mammoths often died in cold places where their bodies were covered in ice and snow. The ice worked like a freezer to save the bodies of these animals. Scientists can even tell what mammoths ate by looking in their stomachs!

All mammoths were plant-eaters. They may have spent up to twenty hours a day eating grass, leaves, and

tree branches. By chewing so much,
a mammoth wore out its teeth. Like
today's elephants, mammoths went
through six sets of teeth in their
lifetime.

Woolly mammoths lived in Europe,

Siberia, and North America during the last ice age. In North America, the ice sheets reached their peak about twenty thousand years ago. Then they began to melt. By ten thousand years ago, no giant mammoths were left on Earth. Neither were many other giant Ice Age mammals, like saber-toothed cats, ground sloths, and giant beavers.

The saber-toothed cat *Smilodon* (SMI-low-don) was a fast runner. It pounced on prey and stabbed it with its dagger-like teeth. *Smilodon* even hunted the huge mammoths.

Giant ground sloths also became extinct. Today a sloth is a small animal that hangs upside down in rain forest treetops. But back then, giant ground sloths didn't climb trees. They could stand on their hind legs and reach the tops of small trees!

No one thinks of beavers as scary animals. But beavers the size of black bears once lived in lakes and ponds. They had enormous teeth that never stopped growing, but they probably didn't build dams or cut down trees like beavers today.

All these animals were extinct by the end of the Ice Age.

6
Disaster Strikes

Imagine more than half the animals
alive today suddenly becoming extinct.
This actually happened five times
during Earth's history. Scientists call
this a mass extinction.

What caused a lot of animals to
become extinct at the same time?
Scientists don't know for sure. Most

think the extinctions were caused by worldwide disasters.

The extreme weather changes of Earth's ice ages probably caused many extinctions. So much water froze that sea levels dropped. Falling seas left ocean animals stranded in the heat of the sun. At the end of each ice age, the ice melted. Then rising seas drowned some animals that lived on land. These changes did not happen all at once. They took thousands of years.

In the case of the dinosaurs, scientists think that an asteroid crashed into the Gulf of Mexico. This caused

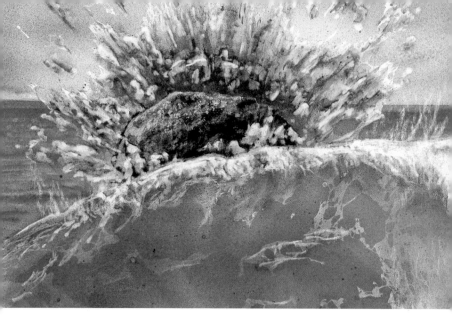

huge tidal waves and fires. Great clouds
of dust and ash blocked out the sun.
The planet cooled down.

Without sunlight, plants died.
Without food, plant-eating dinosaurs
died, too. Finally, the meat-eating
dinosaurs that fed on the plant-eating
dinosaurs died off.

The most recent mass extinction was at the end of the last ice age. During this time, South America and Australia lost most of their large mammals. Almost all the animals that became extinct weighed more than ninety pounds.

Why did so many giant animals die at the end of the Ice Age? After the glaciers melted, the earth warmed. Some of the foods that the giant animals ate may have disappeared. Animals that lived easily in the cold may not have been able to survive when it got warmer.

While the large animals died out, smaller species, like shrews and mice, didn't. Why? One reason is that large animals have fewer babies. And they don't have babies as often as small animals. When there are too few adult animals to have babies, a species won't be around long.

Also large animals need more food, and so they need more space to find food. For example, an area that had enough food for ten mammoths might also have enough to feed ten thousand mice. If weather changes made food harder to find, only one mammoth could live in that area. Meanwhile, a thousand mice could still live there. When a species gets down to just one or two animals, it dies out.

Once people appeared on Earth, they hunted animals to extinction, like the great auk, the dodo, and the Atlantic gray whale. Even when they didn't hunt an animal, people could still hurt its chances of surviving.

When people spread throughout the world, they brought with them animals such as rats and cats. Rats and cats are a threat to birds. They have caused many kinds of birds to die out.

Today, animals go extinct because their homes are destroyed. Logging, clearing rain forests, draining wetlands, introducing diseases, and polluting the environment are all things that harm animal homes. They also hurt the few groups of people who still live in the rain forests. These people live by hunting and gathering like our ancestors did long ago.

Right now, most extinctions come from people destroying rain forests. That's because more different kinds of animals live there than anyplace else.

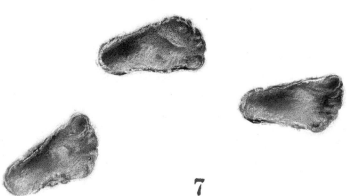

7

Can People Go Extinct?

We always hear about extinct
animals. But did you know humans
can become extinct, too? It happened
a long time ago to the Neanderthals.

Neanderthals lived around 200
thousand years ago. They were a
different species of human than we
are. They were short. They had big

heads and brains larger than ours. For many thousands of years, Neanderthals lived side by side with other humans. But around thirty thousand years ago, these other people evolved into modern people like us. At the same time, Neanderthals died out. No one is quite sure why.

Some scientists think that modern humans had better tools and weapons. Maybe modern people used their weapons to kill the Neanderthals. Or maybe better tools helped modern people survive hard times when the Neanderthals couldn't.

Today there is only one species of human—*Homo sapiens* (HO-mo SA-pee-inz). Africans, Asians, Europeans, Native Americans, and all other people living on Earth are members of the same species. In a way, we are all part of the same human family.

8
Not Too Late

People can cause animals to become extinct. But they can also protect endangered animals. How? Governments are passing laws against hunting animals such as the California gray whale. Zoos are helping to save animals like the panda, the ring-tailed lemur, and the golden lion tamarin.

Kids all over the world help to protect life on Earth by cleaning up beaches and wetlands, planting trees, writing letters to mayors and presidents, and collecting money to help save the rain forests. They know someday this world will be theirs.

There are many happy endings, too. For a while, the bald eagle, the national bird of the United States, was endangered. The pesticide DDT made the eggshells too thin for baby eagles to hatch. By 1963, there were only 417 nesting pairs in the whole country.

After the government banned DDT

in 1973, the birds began to do better.
People all over the country worked to
protect the places where bald eagles
made their nests. By 1995, there were
4,500 nesting pairs of bald eagles in
the U.S. Now they are no longer in
danger.

People can work together to save endangered animals if they care. But if we don't watch out, today's animals may become the strange extinct creatures of tomorrow.

A two-ton beast with a single horn on its nose? A horselike animal with black and white stripes? A giant cat with a golden mane? An animal that walks on two legs and talks? Imagine that!